THIS IS ME!

REFLECTIONS OF SELF

Edited By Roseanna Caswell

First published in Great Britain in 2024 by:

YoungWriters® Est. 1991

Young Writers
Remus House
Coltsfoot Drive
Peterborough
PE2 9BF
Telephone: 01733 890066
Website: www.youngwriters.co.uk

All Rights Reserved
Book Design by Ashley Janson
© Copyright Contributors 2023
Softback ISBN 978-1-83565-132-2

Printed and bound in the UK by BookPrintingUK
Website: www.bookprintinguk.com
YB0577P

FOREWORD

For Young Writers' latest competition This Is Me, we asked primary school pupils to look inside themselves, to think about what makes them unique, and then write a poem about it! They rose to the challenge magnificently and the result is this fantastic collection of poems in a variety of poetic styles.

Here at Young Writers our aim is to encourage creativity in children and to inspire a love of the written word, so it's great to get such an amazing response, with some absolutely fantastic poems. It's important for children to focus on and celebrate themselves and this competition allowed them to write freely and honestly, celebrating what makes them great, expressing their hopes and fears, or simply writing about their favourite things. This Is Me gave them the power of words. The result is a collection of inspirational and moving poems that also showcase their creativity and writing ability.

I'd like to congratulate all the young poets in this anthology, I hope this inspires them to continue with their creative writing.

CONTENTS

Bolton School Junior Boys, Bolton

Anhad Singh Kockhhar (10)	1
Kamran Pitkeathly (7)	2
James Smith (10)	4
Aviraat Waghray (9)	5
William Webster (9)	6
Webster Kundodyiva (7)	7
Zakariya Akiff (7)	8
Ved Bhandary (7)	9
Jake Diver (7)	10
Jayan Prakash (7)	11
Karim Zenalabdin (9)	12
Zaidaan Bagasi (8)	13
George Bailey (7)	14
Rian Khistria (7)	15
Brandon Arhin (7)	16
Abu-Bakr Akbar (7)	17
Oliver Robinson (7)	18
Neil Mishra	19
Yahya Khan (7)	20

Crossgates Primary School, Milnrow

Sophia Pearl Buckley (9)	21
James S (9)	22
Oliver Clarke (9)	24
Charley Young (9)	25
Oliver W (10)	26
Brooke A (10)	27
William Barnes (8)	28
Pearl Crane (9)	29
Isla Cooper (8)	30
Henry Southward (9)	31
Tommy Wood (10)	32

Jacob Hayman (9)	33
Gracie Graham (9)	34
William Taylor-Holmes (9)	35
Harley Thurston (9)	36
Charlie D (9)	37
Lexie Carter (9)	38
Oliver King (8)	39
Lewis McWilliam (8)	40
Cody Shaw (8)	41
Phoebe Hopkins (8)	42
Ruby Brown (8)	43
Thomas Wilkie-Fletcher (8)	44

Tynyrheol Primary School, Llangeinor

Eve Force	45
Esther Quigley (9)	46
Poppie Morgan (9)	48
Taylor Jones (7)	49
Casey-Marie Banfield (10)	50
Ruby-Leigh Byrne (9)	51
Jenson Doak	52
Gethin Banfield (8)	53
Lucas Davies	54
Harry Newland (11)	55
Keelan Riddiford (9)	56
Reuben George	57
Jacob Steele (7)	58
Scarlet Lewis (9)	59
Amy Rose	60
Chase Oldfield (7)	61
Billy Rose (8)	62
Blake Hawkins (8)	63

Wellington School, Ayr

Lucienne Garman-Black (11)	64
Riley Stevenson (11)	66
Luella Hutton (11)	67
Rebecca Black (11)	68
Kyle Jimson (10)	70
Kennedy Richmond (11)	71
Sophia Greenan (11)	72
Eva Crane (11)	73
Erika McLaughlan (11)	74
Murray McAleese	75
Matthew Borthwick (11)	76

Westhill Academy, Westhill

Corinne Docherty	77
Ella Hendry (12)	78
Amelie Cooper (12)	79
Harris Reid (12)	80
Harry Caulfield	81
Molly Bletcher-Gray (12)	82
Francesca Sim (12)	83
Erin Black	84
James Snowie	85
Lewis McKellar (12)	86
Abby Clark (13)	87
Jake Craggs (12)	88
Zoe Blair (11)	89
Scarlett McKenzie (12)	90
Freya Davidson (12)	91
Jensen Vettese	92
Emma Ross (12)	93
Arianna McAllister (12)	94
Erin Mitchell (12)	95
Rachel McKenzie	96
Eva Dillon (13)	97
Daisy Mitchell	98
Rosie McCue	99
Sophia Yeomans (12)	100
Alfie Legge (12)	101
Annabel Duncan	102
Brodey Thomas (12)	103
Eden Craib (12)	104

Lucas Mcintosh (12)	105
Molly O'Sullivan (12)	106
Fraser Mennie	107
Iona Ruby Noble	108
Demi Omitogun (12)	109
Dylan Boardman (12)	110
Jemima Mitchell	111
Aaron Zhaodi Li McKay (12)	112
Scott Donaldson (12)	113
James Grant (12)	114
Aaron Kidd (12)	115
Filip Micak (12)	116
Harley Masson (12)	117
Mylah Forrest (12)	118
Sam Lamont (12)	119
Joe Pirie (11)	120
Emily Gomez (12)	121
Brodie Lawson	122
Dylan Smith (12)	123
Zara Hogg	124
Niall Munro	125
Grace Proud	126
Noah Strand (12)	127
Eliana Svensen (13)	128
Ewan Anderson (12)	129
Caleb Humphrey (12)	130

Whitchurch Primary School, Whitchurch-On-Thames

Poppy Grocott (8)	131
Constance Berrington (11)	132
Pippa Stringer-Smith (10)	134
Reuben Lay-Sans (9)	136
Ella Skelhorn (7)	138
Jay Jennings (8)	139
Hugo Lay-Sans (7)	140
Margaret Campbell (7)	141
Micaela Osan (10)	142
Arthur Gammin (7)	143

York Steiner School, Danesmead

Eva Shepherd (11)	144
Gwen Lavan (11)	146
Honey Stewart (12)	147
George Aston (12)	148
Fynn Cuthell (11)	149
Diego Del Castillo (11)	150
Aleksander O'Brien	151
Sebastian Tuck-Parzanese (12)	152
Arthur Greenbrown (11)	153
Lara Joyce-Rodriguez (11)	154
Eryka Lawson-McMullan	155
Matilda McGorty	156

Ysgol Gynradd Tanygrisiau, Tanygrisiau

Cian Parry (10)	157
Sion Thomas-Humphreys (10)	158
Nora Pitt (7)	160
Jim Bentley (9)	161
Hayleigh Wilson-Jones (10)	162
Aron Jones (11)	163
Emmalayla Bentley (7)	164
Owen Jones (10)	165
Agathe Griffiths-Bell (10)	166
Esi Tomos (9)	167
Evie Streeter (8)	168
Layton Butters (7)	169
Cian O'Callaghan (9)	170
Catrin Hatton (10)	171
James Wakelin (8)	172
Lili Thomas (8)	173
Manawydan Roberts (7)	174
Lucy Wakelin (9)	175

THE POEMS

This Is Me

A. S. K. are my initials
Nistaar is my cheeky little sister
Harry Potter is what I like to read
And it's my mum's favourite indeed
Daddy takes me to my football matches
Saving goals is what I do
In the net is where I play
Nobody is scoring a goal today!
Gill is my favourite cricket player
He hits lots of boundaries and saves them too!
Karate and judo are not for me
Only ball sports are my cup of tea
Car racing games are the best
Having Gran Turismo will make me the greatest
Hugs and kisses are what I like
Always there for my family and I
Retiring to bed at the end of the day
With Eli and Monkey is a comfortable way.

Anhad Singh Kockhhar (10)
Bolton School Junior Boys, Bolton

Video Game Kid!

The first step is to gather together all your ingredients and equipment.
You will need:
A bunny-shaped tin,
10 Maltesers,
Kindness, humour (heaps of it),
Playfulness, camping and sports equipment
And last but not least... one Minecraft cap.

Next, blend two tablespoons of kindness with a pinch or two of playfulness
Add a heaped cup filled with half humour and half cheekiness.
Once the mixture is smooth and there are no lumps or bumps
Pour the mixture into your favourite rabbit-shaped tin.

Bake for 7 years in Bolton.
To complete this recipe decorate your creation with camping and sports equipment,
A Minecraft cap (because I'm video game mad)
And don't forget the 10 crunchy indulgent Maltesers.

Now you are done.
Yummy!

Kamran Pitkeathly (7)
Bolton School Junior Boys, Bolton

My Dog, Poppy

My dog, Poppy, is my best buddy
Big and black and often muddy

She's far too big now to sit on my lap
But she still tries to curl on my knee for a nap

Most of the time she listens to what I say
But most of the time she just wants to play

Ready for our walk, pink collar, jangling tag
Must never forget the important poo bag

Her favourite things are tummy rubs
And tickling her ears
Or bringing us the toys
She's collected over the years

In our family, she is a massive part
And I love her with all my heart.

James Smith (10)
Bolton School Junior Boys, Bolton

Cricket Is Everything!

This is a game called cricket
Where as a bowler, your job is to take wickets
As a top-order batter
It's the runs on the board that matter
Building partnerships with your teammates
Keeping up with the required run rate

Six, four, single, double
The slower ball can get me in trouble
Hook, pull, cut, drive
These are the shots in which I thrive

As I score more runs, I can feel it in my bones
That I am creeping closer to that great milestone
When suddenly, the ball hits the edge of the bat
Then I hear the bowler shout, "Howzthat!"

Aviraat Waghray (9)
Bolton School Junior Boys, Bolton

I Am A Hot Dog

I'm a hot dog sausage
A little bit silly but a lot of fun
I'm made of lots of different things, not just one
Skinny and pink and round at the end
If you wobble me, I'll start to bend

My home is a bun, keeping me safe
Stopping me from rolling all over the place
My hobbies are toppings that make me exciting
I like gaming but I'm not keen on writing!

So this is me
I'd love to have you round for tea
As long as you promise
Not to eat me!

William Webster (9)
Bolton School Junior Boys, Bolton

Webster The Webslinger

First, gather respectfulness, safety, and games
Stir in sports, happiness, kindness adventure
and TTRs
Season with joy, doodles, reading, parties,
and spelling
Add a pinch of hopes, dreams, kisses, fun
and games
Pour in a pool, tickles, happiness and fun animals
Add football, walks, cuddles and energy like a lion
Blend in fun, kindness, games and football
Then warm gently with doughnuts, happiness
and cuddles.

Webster Kundodyiva (7)
Bolton School Junior Boys, Bolton

Amazing Me

First, gather pizza and kindness
Stir in hot chocolate, fun, pudding, cute,
and helpful
Season with maths, running, imagination and
reading
Add a pinch of cat, friendly, sweet and sugar
Pour in a bottle of water and love of the sea
Add pickles and ketchup
Blend in butter, chocolate cake and confidence
Then warm gently with blankets, doughnuts
and delectables.

Zakariya Akiff (7)
Bolton School Junior Boys, Bolton

This Is Unbeatable Me!

First, gather animals and a cricket bat
Stir in magic, bravery and some kindness
Season with sports, board games and energy
Add a pinch of caring, kindness and confidence
Pour in some ocean and land animals
Add some sprinkles of magic and joy
Blend in kind, caring animal which is brave
Then warm gently with a soft, warm, gentle rabbit.

Ved Bhandary (7)
Bolton School Junior Boys, Bolton

Jakeadee

First, gather comfiness and love
Stir in football, maths, English and cheesecake
Season with computer games, hopping
and football
Add a pinch of chocolate cake
Pour in a swimming pool full of sparkling water
Add fun and kindness
Blend in excitement and cleverness, smart
and amazing
Then warm gently with being competitive.

Jake Diver (7)
Bolton School Junior Boys, Bolton

The Great, Amazing Jayan

First, gather go-karting and football
Stir in a bit of astroturf that is soft
Season with energy
Add a pinch of dreams, hopes and adventures
Pour in my favourite Formula 1 car and joyfulness
Add a piece of love
Blend in a piece of sport, running and competitiveness
Then warm gently with kindness.

Jayan Prakash (7)
Bolton School Junior Boys, Bolton

All About Me

I'm funny, I'm smart
But...
Being humble is not my strongest part
In school or playing sports
I'm not a losing sort
Playing games, I'm not very patient
Doing equations, I always lose my patience
This homework is inhumane
And writing this homework drove me insane!

Karim Zenalabdin (9)
Bolton School Junior Boys, Bolton

Fantastic Me

First, gather cycling and adventures
Stir in happiness and games
Season with toys and parties
Add a pinch of hopes and dreams
Pour in a lake full of joyfulness, tickles and walks
Blend in boxing, running, cuddles and football
Then warm gently with wonderful cuddles.

Zaidaan Bagasi (8)
Bolton School Junior Boys, Bolton

How To Make Me

First, gather calm and good
Stir in two cats and chocolate bars
Season with TTRs and doodle maths
Add a pinch of happiness and tickles
Pour in a hat full of swimming pool
Add some cuddles
Blend in Mummy and Daddy and kisses
Then warm gently with doughnuts.

George Bailey (7)
Bolton School Junior Boys, Bolton

The Great Me

First, gather football and fun
Stir in my Lego and me
Season with Fortnite and Minecraft
Add a pinch of energy
Pour in a puddle of chocolate
Add sweets and sprinkles
Blend in kindness, love and helpfulness
Then warm gently with making kindness.

Rian Khistria (7)
Bolton School Junior Boys, Bolton

Things I Love Recipe

First, gather kindness and fun
Stir in football and games
Season with summer holidays
Add a pinch of parties
Pour in a river full of friendliness
Add sweets and cake
Blend in dogs, cats, energy and trust
Then warm gently with ice cream.

Brandon Arhin (7)
Bolton School Junior Boys, Bolton

This Is Me

First, gather my cousin and me
Stir in Fortnite
Season with cricket
Add a pinch of basketball
Pour in a swimming pool full of fun
Add sweet cake
Blend in helpfulness, angriness,
unhappiness and cute
Then warm gently in the oven.

Abu-Bakr Akbar (7)
Bolton School Junior Boys, Bolton

How To Make Me

First, gather football and tickles
Stir in lots of football goals
Season with TTRs
Add a pinch of tickles and football
Pour in a lake full of happiness
Add a fluffy dog
Blend in fluffy and lazing pets
Then warm gently with football.

Oliver Robinson (7)
Bolton School Junior Boys, Bolton

This Is Me

First, gather kindness and caring
Stir in chocolate and cake
Season with doodle maths and TTRs
Add a pinch of kindness
Pour in sugar like chocolate
Blend in friendship and hopes, worthiness and cool
Then warm gently with thinking.

Neil Mishra
Bolton School Junior Boys, Bolton

Amazing Me

First, gather footballs and cones
Stir in happiness and kindness
Season with dribbing
Add a pinch of adventure
Pour in dreams and hopes
Blend in energy and laughter, running and jumping
Then warm gently with a hyperactive whisk.

Yahya Khan (7)
Bolton School Junior Boys, Bolton

This Is Me!

How to create me:
A dash of fun
A touch of pepperoni pizza
A sprinkle of sassiness
A teaspoon of kindness
9g of chattiness
2 Squishmallows

Now you need to:
Add the fun and the pizza together
Mix, mix, mix
Then apply kindness
Mix, mix, mix
Spread the sassiness
Mix, mix, mix
Sieve the chattiness
Mix, mix, mix
Drizzle the Squishmallows on
Then, finally...
Mix, mix, mix
This is me! Enjoy!

Sophia Pearl Buckley (9)
Crossgates Primary School, Milnrow

A Recipe For A Nine-Year-Old James

To create a nine-year-old James, you will need:
Jack and Jessica and Mum and Dad
An author, game designer and an office worker
2 McDonald's Happy Meals
With 2 sweet and sour dips, Fruit Shoot
and Diet Coke
A comic book
A picture of Napoleon
Diary of a Wimpy Kid: The Long Haul
A game
A picture of a planet
Water
YouTuber merch
A song from Imagine Dragons
A bottle of Pepsi Max

Now you need to:
Add a tablespoon of Jack
Another tablespoon but with Jessica
Add a tablespoon of Mum

Add a tablespoon of Dad
Now add a picture of Napoleon
Then add a song by Imagine Dragons
Now pour your Pepsi
Add 3lbs of authors
And 10lbs of game designers
Now 60lbs of office workers
Then 2 McDonald's Happy Meals
Add 2 sweet and sour dips
And a Fruit Shoot and Diet Coke
Now add a comic
Then YouTuber merch
Now a picture of a planet
Cook until blue bubbles are visible
Then pour in a bottle of water
Then you have a nine-year-old James.

James S (9)
Crossgates Primary School, Milnrow

All About Me!

Oliver is my name

I love running
My uncle likes drumming
I'm a really cool dude
My sister is rude

I love history, especially the Iron Age
Now watch me perform history on stage

All my friends are silly
Especially Billy

Maths is good
Finished it in a thud
My hand went up in the air
The teacher doesn't care

AC-DC is my thing
And how their songs fly by like a swing.

Oliver Clarke (9)
Crossgates Primary School, Milnrow

This Is Me!

I am sassy but a little bit chatty
I am a girl with long brown hair
I am strong and brave like a wave
I have a dog called Trinny
She is small and skinny
My favourite subject is art
Even though I find it tricky
I'm funny and I love food
I've got sky-blue eyes
I'm full of surprises
This is me!

Charley Young (9)
Crossgates Primary School, Milnrow

This Is Me!

T he family is amazing
H aving many fun times with my amazing brother
I love my big brother
S easide is my favourite place to go

I love my cat
S ometimes I talk to my mum when I need to

M e and my family have so much fun together
E verything is alright when I play with my friend.

Oliver W (10)
Crossgates Primary School, Milnrow

This Is Me!

My name is Brooke
I like to read books
I am good at gymnastics
That's why I like to do back tucks
My eyes are like the ocean blue
Sparkling like diamonds, this is true
My hair is as blonde as the beaming sun
I love to laugh and have lots of fun
Many talents I possess
B.R.O.O.K.E is the best!
This is me!

Brooke A (10)
Crossgates Primary School, Milnrow

This Is Me

I'm a controller in a Minecraft game
I am a dolphin swimming freely in the
Atlantic Ocean
I'm as kind as God Himself
I'm as cold as an iceberg, yet as warm as lava
I'm so cool, you're so cool, we're all so cool!
I'm so cool, I rock this planet called Earth
You're so cool, I drool, yeah.

William Barnes (8)
Crossgates Primary School, Milnrow

This Is Me!

I am as kind as a rose
I am a horse lover
I have eyes as blue as the sky
My hair is as blonde as white chocolate
I am fast like a lion
I am always hungry
My favourite food is pancakes
I'm a deep sleeper
I'm always performing at shows
And winning rosettes at my favourite place to go
This is me.

Pearl Crane (9)
Crossgates Primary School, Milnrow

All About Me

My name is Isla
It rhymes with Lyla
I find maths cool
And I also like pool
I don't have a favourite food
But listen to me, dude
My friend is Evie
And she is not a meanie
I sometimes play fight with my dad
And it sometimes makes me sad
My mum smells nice
Not like rice.

Isla Cooper (8)
Crossgates Primary School, Milnrow

I Am Me

I am as quick as Sonic
My hidden talent is naming countries and flags
My eyes are as blue as the sea
I'm funny, supportive and helpful
My brother loves me
I love my family
I'm as brave as a tiger
I'm nine years old
My favourite author is Tom Fletcher
I am Hero Henry.

Henry Southward (9)
Crossgates Primary School, Milnrow

Me And Just Me!

T he sister I have is annoying
H our or two of Fortnite
I am a boy
S uper big slab of pizza that I love

I am ten years old
S ometimes I get in trouble

M y gaming skills need to be perfect
E xercise for two hours a day.

Tommy Wood (10)
Crossgates Primary School, Milnrow

This Is Me

T he team for me is Man United
H elping others
I love my mum
S it in the front seat

I love Coca-Cola
S tarbucks, I go there a lot

M y favourite food is a Big Mac
E ggs are my favourite protein.

Jacob Hayman (9)
Crossgates Primary School, Milnrow

This Is Me

T eamwork makes the dream work
H appy every day
I nside is fun
S cience is the best

I n PE, we have fun
S liding is so much fun

M y dog, rabbit and puppy are the best
E lsa is my best friend.

Gracie Graham (9)
Crossgates Primary School, Milnrow

This Is Me

W illiam is my name
I have friends so my job is to be kind
L ibby is someone I know
L ove space, okay?
I love elephant football
A boy who can go to school
M y emotions sometimes go bang!

William Taylor-Holmes (9)
Crossgates Primary School, Milnrow

This Is Me!

I am fast with a cast
My eyes are as blue as the wide, open sky
My hair is blonde
I have four brothers and a sister
I have a nice family
I am as kind as a doctor helping their patients
I am fearless like a lion
This is me!

Harley Thurston (9)
Crossgates Primary School, Milnrow

This Is Me!

C aring
H appy to help
A great reader
R eally good at football
L ove my family and friends
I like maths
E veryone is my friend.

Charlie D (9)
Crossgates Primary School, Milnrow

This Is Me

L ove to ride horses every day
E njoy chips when I play
X mas is my favourite time of year
I am a cottage pie lover
E njoy eating pizza.

Lexie Carter (9)
Crossgates Primary School, Milnrow

This Is Me

G ames are my thing
A nime is the best
M inecraft drips
E xtra game time, please
R eading is good, though not just on screens.

Oliver King (8)
Crossgates Primary School, Milnrow

This Is What I Like

Lewis is my name
Football is my game
YouTube is my thing
I like chicken wings
I have lots of favourite drinks
I brush my teeth at the sink.

Lewis McWilliam (8)
Crossgates Primary School, Milnrow

This Is Me

C olouring is my favourite
O ranges are the best
D inosaurs are the best and I play with them
Y oghurts are yummy.

Cody Shaw (8)
Crossgates Primary School, Milnrow

How To Make Me

A bit of happiness
1 book
A lot of kindness
Extra Taylor Swift
A cute cat
Bits of pink
1 lipstick
1 pizza
Enjoy!

Phoebe Hopkins (8)
Crossgates Primary School, Milnrow

How To Make Ruby

First, get a bowl
Add 10 pieces of pizza
Add some syrup
Then a dash of fun
And you have made me!

Ruby Brown (8)
Crossgates Primary School, Milnrow

This Is Me

A sprinkle of funny
A jug of kind
Some pepperoni pizza
A bucket of helpful
A sprinkle of help.

Thomas Wilkie-Fletcher (8)
Crossgates Primary School, Milnrow

What Makes Me, Me

My eyes glisten as blue as the sky
They will never ever tell a lie
My skin is as white as the snow
In the dark, you can see it glow

My favourite place to go is the beach
I love it when people say, "You're too tall to reach!"
On Sundays, I love to play
In my bed, I enjoy to lay

I look adorable in a bright blue bow
At school, I like to put on a show
My loving, caring mum is as beautiful as a rose
To make me laugh she will tickle my nose

My perfect fluffy furry cat
When she's outside she likes to hunt for a rat
My cat is as sweet as cotton candy
Having a cat in the house is quite handy.

Eve Force
Tynyrheol Primary School, Llangeinor

This Is Me

I love to watch a stunning sunset
Always, on a weekend, so I will never forget
Being at the beach is my favourite space
As it helps my mind escape to a glorious place

I'm as fast as a lion on a rugby pitch
At the end of a game, I look like I have gone down a ditch
My sister is the biggest fan
Even though she doesn't get a tan

My fabulous friend and I play on our phones
My sister hates it and loves to moan
Facetime is a great way to stay in touch
Night-time matters can get way too much

My best days are at the swimming pool
The ones with slides are really cool
In the water, I'm a slippery snake
For a treat after I enjoy a slice of cake

My favourite animal resides in trees
They love to hang and sway in the breeze

Did you know that sloths have no gender
Under extinction, they desperately need a defender

Curly, crazy chestnut hair
I often have no clue what to wear
My biggest passion is to draw
Sometimes I do so much my hand starts to get very sore.

Esther Quigley (9)
Tynyrheol Primary School, Llangeinor

This Is Who I'm Meant To Be

I have long luscious blonde locks
And enjoy pleasant peaceful long walks
My ambition is a burning flame
Appearing on YouTube is my famous claim

At the beach, I enjoy to play
On the shimmering shiny sand, I love to lay
I adore watching the sunset
At the beach I never get upset

My best friend is my cute cuddly dog
He can jump so high like a leaping frog
His smooth soft coat is coloured cream
Just like me, he loves to sleep and dream

I am a rainbow of emotions
And I enjoy using my imagination
Spending time with the people I care for
Is just important as my love to draw.

Poppie Morgan (9)
Tynyrheol Primary School, Llangeinor

Polar Bear

P olar bears are cute kittens that live in the snow
O n the snow, there is incredible ice where polar bears live
L ive in the now, because if they go in the heat they will be too hot
A polar bear is a white bear that lives in the snow
R eal polar bears live in cold climates

B e a polar bear, if you are a polar bear, a very good polar bear
E ven though polar bears are good creatures, they can be mean like a lion
A nd it is a cute bear that lives in the winter and in the summer
R eal bears in the world, creatures of the world.

Taylor Jones (7)
Tynyrheol Primary School, Llangeinor

What Makes Me Special

I am one of a kind
I have a terrifically intelligent mind
My eyes shimmer in the sun
When we go out, I always call shotgun

I love the sound of relentless rain
It's soothing when it's bashing on the windowpane
Monday morning I'm really tired
By Friday I'm exceptionally wired

Long calming walks on the beach
I hate it when birds scream and screech
I enjoy playing on the smooth, soft sand
While my sister gets tanned

Hungry as a bear waking in spring
Ravenous, I'll eat anything
My favourite dog is my friend, Sky
When I fall, she comforts me, so I don't cry.

Casey-Marie Banfield (10)
Tynyrheol Primary School, Llangeinor

This Is Me

T his is me! My name is Ruby. I am smart and I like swimming

H ere is my favourite animal. My favourite animal is a koala

I really like it when I go on holiday

S peaking of smart, my sister is smart like an elephant

I have one brother and two sisters. They are very balmy!

S ister One is cool and smart. Sister Two is cool and small

M y sister, Lacey, is 12 and my other sister, Penny is 3. My brother, Tommy, is 2.

E aster is my favourite time because I get to eat a lot of chocolate.

Ruby-Leigh Byrne (9)
Tynyrheol Primary School, Llangeinor

What Makes Me Unique

I am a star at football
On the pitch, you hear me call
My feet slither like a snake
After a game, I like to eat cake

I enjoy playing on my phone
I like to eat ice cream cones
I love to cosy up in my comfy bed
My favourite colour is ruby red

My family are loving, caring and loyal
My grandfather is from the royal family
I like to eat so much cake
And when I'm done, I get a stomachache.

Jenson Doak
Tynyrheol Primary School, Llangeinor

This Is Me

My eyes glisten like the oceans
Deep down I have so many emotions
I am slippery like a snake
One of my favourite things to do is bake

I love to play the game football
Jake, my best friend, I love to call
While I play on my phone
My dog digs to hide her bone

Outside I like to play with my toy gun
While my sisters jump and have lots of fun
I enjoy playing with my dog in the park
When she has fun, she really starts to bark.

Gethin Banfield (8)
Tynyrheol Primary School, Llangeinor

This Is Me

My eyes are gleaming sapphires in the sky
It is not very often you will see me cry
As fast as a cheetah I can run
Improved all the running I have done
My dad is one of a kind
When I misbehave, he can lose his mind
I love it when we go on a trip
When I go to Cornwall, I love to have a dip
My family is important to me
I love it when we all sit down to tea
Fun, friendly family time
I'm so proud that they are mine.

Lucas Davies
Tynyrheol Primary School, Llangeinor

Hedgehog

H arry's favourite animal is a hedgehog
E very hedgehog devours like an earwig
D o not touch a hedgehog when it is in a ball
G reat hedgehogs
E arwigs are as small as a centipede
H edgehogs are spiker than a spiky ball
O utside they like to live in lovely bushes
G ood-looking hedgehogs are a wonderful thing to witness.

Harry Newland (11)
Tynyrheol Primary School, Llangeinor

Sports

S port is an exercise that is exciting for you to play
P articipants play in every game that you play
O bviously a new sport for you
R ecovery can be used in any sport, recovering is a passion
T ackle any player you want but don't be down and dirty
S mashing into many other people who are so injured and can hurt you.

Keelan Riddiford (9)
Tynyrheol Primary School, Llangeinor

Scientist

S cientists are very smart
C reative smart scientists
I ntelligent making potions
E quipment such as glass tubes
N ew scientists have to learn
T eal potions are shiny
I ntelligent scientists are smart
S eeing through the goggles, they look like spies
T est tubes are for explosions.

Reuben George
Tynyrheol Primary School, Llangeinor

Spaniels

S paniels are cute like a cat
P layful Spaniels like to jump
A nd Spaniels are fast runners
N oisy Spaniels bark loudly like thunder
I ncredible Spaniels, loving Spaniels like to cuddle
E very Spaniel likes to have a nice walk
L onely, lovely Spaniels are sad
S paniels like to eat a lot.

Jacob Steele (7)
Tynyrheol Primary School, Llangeinor

Meerkats

M eerkats are funny like cloudy clowns
E very time I see a meerkat it makes me joyful
E very meerkat is the cutest animal on Earth
R esting and relaxing on a log
K eepers look after meerkats kindly
A dmire the powerful meerkats
T ame a meerkat, they are adorable.

Scarlet Lewis (9)
Tynyrheol Primary School, Llangeinor

This Is Me!

T his is me
H ere are my emotions
I 'm as angry as a dragon
S ometimes I am as happy as a daisy

I am as calm as a burnt-out fire
S miling all day long

M y raging fire - angry feelings
E njoying everything every day.

Amy Rose
Tynyrheol Primary School, Llangeinor

Kittens

K ittens are cute
I like kittens because they are fluffy
T hey are very playful
T hey are strong and can jump super high like a big dog
E at loads of fabulous favourite food
N osy like a baby kitten.

Chase Oldfield (7)
Tynyrheol Primary School, Llangeinor

Billy R

B ig, brave, buff, big brain Billy
I ntelligent like a chimp
L ong slithering hair like a snake
L oving as much as a koala
Y es, I am a bodybuilder

R aging dragon when annoyed.

Billy Rose (8)
Tynyrheol Primary School, Llangeinor

Rugby

R ugby is the best
U pon every touch, you turn over the ball
G et tons of tackles to win
B est team is Tondu, as strong as rock
Y elling at me to get everyone back.

Blake Hawkins (8)
Tynyrheol Primary School, Llangeinor

Halloween Is The Best Holiday

H alloween is the best holiday
A llowing us to have lots of sweets
L oving every bite
L oving that it's night
O ctober is the time we do it
W e all have a great time together whilst we scare those who are unaware
E erie shadows lurking about
E vening is when children come around
N ot having a care about cavities

I s the spirit still here?
S tillness in your cafe here

T he leaves are blowing about
H e creeps around the corner
E nchanted stories being told

B e very scared you should be
E vil scary costumes
S pooky, scary skeletons
T errors the children are when too many sweets they are handed.

Lucienne Garman-Black (11)
Wellington School, Ayr

What Is It?

Teams all over the world compete
Many people try to get a seat
And a lot of the time you can sneak a treat
Many people call it a rough sport
Or many other names of sorts
You never get a nil-nil game
And many club teams have an odd name

People may call it egg-chasing
But I just like how they are always racing
Scores are odd
And there are twenty-three in the squad
Some of the stadiums even look like a pod
Five for a try
Whilst a conversion gets booted in the sky

This was a marvellous creation
As every nation
Competes for the trophy
What is it?

Answer: Rugby.

Riley Stevenson (11)
Wellington School, Ayr

This Is Me

I love my dog, his name is Chase
I think Rangers are totally ace
My family is glam
Shopping is my jam
Netball and hockey are my chance
I love to sleep and Shaun the Sheep

I don't like bees, they break my knees
I don't like salmon or gammon
I wouldn't even eat it in a famine
I don't like school and rain
Getting up in the morning is a pain

I'm funny and sassy
And a Scottish lassie
I love to complain
My brothers are a pain
I wish they would flee
This is me!

Luella Hutton (11)
Wellington School, Ayr

Me In Many Ways

I love my pets
I love to go flying on jets
I think I'm funny but I'm always chatty
I love parties
I love my friends
I always keep up with the new trends
I think I'm intelligent but I'm not that sure
I love my cat's purr
I love having fun
While my dogs are out on a run
I'm quite smart
I have a big heart
I'm always picky
I dread being sixty
There are some people I dislike
I love riding my bike
I love my fam
I miss out on all the glam
I love rugby

I want a pet monkey
I hate tea
I am me.

Rebecca Black (11)
Wellington School, Ayr

Parent Problems

My dad's too fat to hit me with a bat
My mum is always trying not to be crying
My brothers are always happy because if not,
they are all unhappy
Me, I'm always laughing, or my feelings, they
are gaffing

School is my hiding place
My place I decree
My place to be free
My place to be me

My parents always shout
I tell them not to shout but they never hear me out
I use lots of tissue because I have lots of issues
I have parental problems.

Kyle Jimson (10)
Wellington School, Ayr

Food

A slab of cheesy pizza, give me that on a plate
But don't give me vegetables, for those I do hate
A chocolate bar an iconic design
Caramel is great, it is quite divine
Burgers, exquisite, especially with cheese
Slushies are the best, they give me brain freeze
Churros, full of sugar, perfect as can be
But tomatoes, the worst, they belong in the sea
To finish, sweets, excellent, top-of-the-line
And cake, I would rate it 9/9.

Kennedy Richmond (11)
Wellington School, Ayr

This Is Me

Sometimes sweet
Sometimes merry
My favourite fruit is a strawberry
I don't like milk
I don't like tea
Isn't it great to be me?

I'm a huge Celtic fan
I don't like the make-up ban
I love my friends and my fam
I love shopping and looking glam

My dog, Piper, is very hyper
And she likes to eat all the spiders
I love a good rant
And so does my aunt

This is me!

Sophia Greenan (11)
Wellington School, Ayr

This Is Me

I am brave
I am kind
But sometimes angry of another kind
I love my dog
I am sassy as can be
I am me

I hate cheese
I hate rain
I hate salmon
I hate when people try to force me to eat it
It makes me want to throw a fit
I am me

I am dramatic
I am happy
I love dancing and acting
I am silly
I am caring and kind
I love my family beyond infinity
I am me.

Eva Crane (11)
Wellington School, Ayr

All About Me

I can be sweet
I can be sour
Horse riding is my power
I love those jump wings and poles
And also those Flump marshmallows

Mac and cheese is not my thing
But I do like a bit of bling
Also, add some pink in
Shopping is my favourite thing
Can't forget Ikea
Make-up, skincare and clothes
Are only some of my favourite things.

Erika McLaughlan (11)
Wellington School, Ayr

Halloween

H alloween is my jam
A nd sweets are my treats
L aughing is my trick
L ollies I love to lick
O ver my face, the chocolate will stick
W ill I still be able to walk?
E ven with all these sweets in my tum
E mpty bucket of sweets my life complete
N othing left to eat as my sweet treat.

Murray McAleese
Wellington School, Ayr

Special

You are...

- **S** pecial to everyone who loves you
- **P** erfect, in your own way
- **E** nlightened in every way
- **C** reative in the best ways possible
- **I** ntelligent, like Einstein
- **A** mazing, by being yourself
- **L** oved in every way possible

... in every way possible!

Matthew Borthwick (11)
Wellington School, Ayr

A Recipe For My Dog, Cooper

First, gather intelligence and an appetite for anything but dog food
Then, break up the lingering smell of dog breath in your utility room
Season with love for jumping in a lake then getting in your freshly cleaned car
Add a pinch of more hugs and kisses for your grandparents than you
Poor in a bathtub worth of slobber
And an ocean worth of needing to pee at 2am
Fold in puppy eyes and food and a grey beard
Then, warm gently by ripping up all the money spent on dog toys
Take out and leave for fifteen minutes while you remember you forgot to pick up dog food
Then, gaze into those big, black beautiful eyes and realise that everything you do for him is worth it.

Corinne Docherty
Westhill Academy, Westhill

A Recipe For My Ferret, Winter

First, gather summer days playing and winter night cuddles
Stir in a galaxy of extravagant adventures
Marinade on foggy days leading to endless laughter and fun
Pour in a world of trust, tickles and triumphant victories
When racing in the back garden
Toss in a chunk of bravery when stealing toys and socks
Whip and then infuse careless evenings and early mornings
Drizzle in lots of happy jumps and getting covered in dirt after digging
Whisk a tablespoon of sniffs, falls and licks into it
And sprinkle in fresh snow and cold paws
Finally, sauté in warm walks in a bright blue harness.

Ella Hendry (12)
Westhill Academy, Westhill

A Recipe For My Brother, Dylan

First, gather a lot of trust and respect to make us feel happy and safe
Next, stir in lots of love to make us feel active and to share lots of love with our friends and family
Add a pinch of sharing our stuff to make us trust each other and feel we are best friends
Add a whip of mountain biking at Ballater to spend lots of time together
Flood the whole world with laughs, giggles and jokes to make each other smile for the rest of the day
And share how much of a generous brother he is
Sieve in a world full of kindness, care and loads of joy
Finally, warm the tastiest, yummiest cake, by sharing love with our family.

Amelie Cooper (12)
Westhill Academy, Westhill

A Recipe For Myself

First, gather helpfulness and funny jokes
Stir in dirt bikes and video games with my phone and my PS5
Season with football and table tennis
With the joy of life and having great friends
Add a pinch of sharing and caring
Pour in going to the cinema and reading with lots of judo
With bravery and knowing I am loved
Blend my favourite apps such as YouTube and TikTok
Going to the park and playing with my friends
Powered by tasty food and drinks
Then warm gently, by friends and family.

Harris Reid (12)
Westhill Academy, Westhill

A Recipe For My Dog, Leo

First, gather their cuteness and their love
for cuddles
Stir in their love for our family
And of course, some sleep
Seasoned with a sprinkle of walks
Make sure to add a bit of the mentality of a player
And a couple of drops of licks and kisses
With quite a lot of happy memories
Mix that with a lot, and I mean a lot, of digging
holes in our back garden
Then mix and warm gently, by saying 'treat'
six times
Then you have the final result
My dog, Leo.

Harry Caulfield
Westhill Academy, Westhill

My Fat Cat, Russell

First, gather loads of fatness and food
Next, stir in a giant box of yummy, delicious spiders
Season with lots of amazing killing adventures
Add a big pinch of lovely tickles and
amazing kisses
Pour in a giant cloud's worth of fluffiness and lots
of chunkiness
Don't forget loads of bites and lovely toys
Blend squeaking and craziness, stretching
and sleeping
Then warm up gently by playing with a small
laser pointer making him go stupid.

Molly Bletcher-Gray (12)
Westhill Academy, Westhill

A Poem About My Grandma

(This poem is dedicated to my wonderful grandma who I lost a few years ago.)

First, gather creativeness and kindness and a lot of funniness
Stir in a gallon of imagination and making creations
Season with a lot of joy
Add a pinch of sprinkles for wackiness, laughter and wonderfulness
Pour in a sunbeam of determination and positivity
And a bit of elegance and remembrance from us at home who miss you loads and loads
Blend in some heart-warming memories
Warm with tender goodbyes, rest in peace, my extraordinary grandma.

Francesca Sim (12)
Westhill Academy, Westhill

My Little Ratty Dog

First, you will need to gather 3 tablespoons
of silliness and family love
Next, you'll need to stir in a cup of balls
After all that, blend in a few games and walks
Then get a slice of playing with other crazy
dogs into the mixture
Pour in an ocean-sized amount of food
And a little pinch of dumbness and calmness
Blend in a small amount of kisses and cuddles
Warm with gentle words 'walks' and 'sleep time'.

Erin Black
Westhill Academy, Westhill

My Poem About Michael

First, gather a pot full of silliness
And a spoonful of frizz
Stir in some friends and family
Season with intelligence and football
Add a pinch of Fortnite
Pour in an ocean's worth of basketball
And a bowl full of making Rory
Make weird noises in PSE
Stir in going out with friends
And playing football at Carnie
Then warm gently by playing basketball
At the Crombie MUGA.

James Snowie
Westhill Academy, Westhill

This Is Me

First, gather football and clumsiness
Stir in a lot of laughs and giggles
Season with friends and family
Add a pinch of mountain biking and bravery
Pour in FIFA, adventures, and crazy memories
Blend happiness and intelligence
Then warm gently by adding funny times with my friends
Mix in Westdyke Community Club and Tottenham Hotspur
Then finish it off with Aberdeen FC.

Lewis McKellar (12)
Westhill Academy, Westhill

This Is Eva

First, gather kindness and bravery
Stir with a lot of being mean and watching TV
Season with a love for horses and dancing
Add a pinch of playing video games and eating food
Pour in some craziness and cuddles with the dog, Dave
Add me then blend in being funny and creativity
Drawing, her friends, hugs and her mental laughs
Then warm gently with the care for her loved ones.

Abby Clark (13)
Westhill Academy, Westhill

A Recipe For My Guinea Pig, Cookie

First, gather cuteness and mischievousness
Stir in bags of lettuce, add that to the list
Season with bites on the finger mistaken for food
Add a pinch of energy when you're in a good mood
Pour in the cosy to have a good nap
And a desire for cuddles while sitting on my lap
Blend being frightened by the sound of fireworks
Then warm gently by knowing you'll be remembered.

Jake Craggs (12)
Westhill Academy, Westhill

My Hamster, Oreo

First, gather adorable and fluffy
Then stir in cute and cuddly
Season with a sleepy furball
Add a pinch of running in his ball
Pour in how he is oh, so calming
And how he loves sleeping
Blend his climbing and chewing
Also his sniffing and eating
Then warm gently, by adding his cute kisses
And his happiness is one of my only wishes
I love you Oreo and I always will.

Zoe Blair (11)
Westhill Academy, Westhill

A Recipe For My Auntie's Cat, Loki

First, gather a bit of curiosity and love for food
Stir in some cuddles and snuggles
Season with hiking and exploration
Add a pinch of thinking she's a god
Pour in an abundance of hunting birds and vermin
And a hatred of anyone that's really loud
Blend in a warm generosity for giving you dead things
Then warm by giving a very generous number of treats.

Scarlett McKenzie (12)
Westhill Academy, Westhill

Recipe For Axel, My Cavapoo Puppy

First, gather curiosity and playfulness
Stir in lots of tasteful treats
Season with one hundred slobbery stolen socks
Add a pinch of zoomies and going crazy
Pour in a cup of scrumptious cocktail sausages
Add a gallon of cuddles, kisses, and love
Blend in some chewed-up toys, sniffing and running around
Then heat with the sound of that favourite word 'walkies'!

Freya Davidson (12)
Westhill Academy, Westhill

This Is Me

First, gather worries and love
Stir in a bowl of video games and tuna
Season with imagination and creativity
Add a pinch of kindness and a tiny bit of anger issues
Pour in a bucket of laughter
And a book for reading and extra flavour
Then blend some writing, chocolate, animals and some gravy
Then warm it up with a warm toasty bed
And then you are done.

Jensen Vettese
Westhill Academy, Westhill

A Recipe For My Brother

First, gather lots of happiness and funniness
Stir in some loudness, an Xbox and an iPad
Season with fearlessness and lots of adventures
Add a pinch of silliness and light blonde hair
Pour in a river of basketballs and footballs
And games, love and lots and lots of care
Blend in some hugs, dreams and drama queen
Then warm gently by being the best brother ever.

Emma Ross (12)
Westhill Academy, Westhill

A Recipe For Me!

First, gather dreams and parties
Stir in some cheer and dancing
Season with some kindness and helpfulness
Add a pinch of family and friends
Pour in a lifetime of adventures
Then boil with some artistic pictures
And holding handstands in gymnastics
Blend in a mixture of funniness and caringness
Then to finish, loads of sweeties and sleepovers.

Arianna McAllister (12)
Westhill Academy, Westhill

A Recipe For My Dog, Hank

First, gather braveness and sleepiness
Stir in a pile of stones
Season with cheese and ham
Add a pinch of happiness
Pour in a bunch of calming energy
And make sure to add in swimming
Blend tummy rubs and laziness
Intelligence, slobbers and don't forget love
Then warm gently, by showing you care
And love him with your whole heart.

Erin Mitchell (12)
Westhill Academy, Westhill

Bowmore

First, gather happiness and playfulness
Stir in some walks, treats, and tummy rubs
Season with Doggy Dreams
Add a pinch of jumping on the sofa
Pour in car journeys and barking
Add more kisses and cuddles blankets and bubbles, sleeping and weeping
Then walkies and dreamies
Then warm gently with baths.

Rachel McKenzie
Westhill Academy, Westhill

Abby

First, gather love and trustworthiness
Stir in Dave, loving and cuddles
Season with some dancing and lazing on the sofa
Add a pinch of sassiness
Pour in a world's worth of loyalty
And some craziness and funniness
Blend snacks, horses, hope and happiness
Then warm gently by saying, "I will always be by your side."

Eva Dillon (13)
Westhill Academy, Westhill

A Recipe For Jemima

First, gather creativity and love
Stir in a pot of favourite dance moves
Season with a splash of Taylor Swift songs
Add a pinch of her love of flowers
Pour in a pint of thoughtfulness and generosity
Add a plate of her love of Vikings
Blend eating and football and drawing and netball
Then warm gently with her family and friends.

Daisy Mitchell
Westhill Academy, Westhill

A Recipe For My Hedgehog

First, gather some spikes and fluff
Stir in his blanket so he doesn't go spiky
Season with love and lots of cuddles
Add a pinch of tugging or even some running
Pour in a humungous bath
And lots and lots of squirming bugs
Blend some nerves, huffing and puffing
Then warm gently by saying, "It's time for bed."

Rosie McCue
Westhill Academy, Westhill

A Recipe For My Cousin, Alex

First, gather silliness and humour
Stir in a tub of talkative
Season with playful and cuteness
Add a pinch of loudness mixed with superheroes
Pour in a sea of imagination
And 5 litres of running around
Blend stories, shouting and sweetness
Then gently warm by shouting
"What are you doing here?"
And enjoy.

Sophia Yeomans (12)
Westhill Academy, Westhill

A Recipe For Myself

First, acquire intelligence and hot-headedness
Stir in a divot full of video games
Season with a whole new world of books
Add a pinch of colours and scenery
Pour in a galaxy-sized amount of movies
And a sound-breaking amount of music
Blend hours and hours of sleep
Then warm gently, by filling the universe
with kindness.

Alfie Legge (12)
Westhill Academy, Westhill

A Recipe For My Doggy

First, gather playfulness and craziness
Stir in tummy rubs, cuddles and treats
Season with a bit of cuteness and kisses
Add a pinch of zoomies
Pour in walkies and sprinkle on some dinner time
Blend in teddies, tickles, sniffles and snuggles
Then warm gently by topping it off with car rides
And eating food that is not his.

Annabel Duncan
Westhill Academy, Westhill

Recipe For My Parrot, Papu

First, gather string and foolishness
Stir in a tub of his favourite toys
Season with a cunning personality and intelligence
Add a pinch of hatred towards dogs
Pour in an ocean's worth of balls and pumpkin toys
And trust within me and my family
Then blend with adventures and treats
Then warm with a game of tug of war.

Brodey Thomas (12)
Westhill Academy, Westhill

A Recipe For My Dog, Oscar

First, gather strength and activeness
Stir in some sharp teeth
Season with tummy rubs
Add a pinch of playfulness
Pour in a lot of love for food
And some brains with a pinch of laziness
Blend biting and loudness, fun and sleeping
Then warm gently by going to the beach.

Eden Craib (12)
Westhill Academy, Westhill

A Recipe For My Cat, Casper

First, gather snow and googly eyes
Stir in kindness and many silly things
Season with cuteness then flops
Add a pinch of annoyance and treats
Pour in infinite amounts of energy
And a dash of speed
Blend noisiness, and enough fur to even keep a naked yeti warm
Then warm gently by snuggles and chasing people.

Lucas Mcintosh (12)
Westhill Academy, Westhill

A Recipe For My Cats

In a bowl add:
200g of overly expensive cat food
200g of catnip
4tbs of playful biting
200g moodiness
10g of playful licking

Mix until you have a smooth, soft batter
Pour in a mountain of loyalty while stirring
Warm in the oven for 3 minutes
Add a glaze of snuggles and nuzzling over top.

Molly O'Sullivan (12)
Westhill Academy, Westhill

A Recipe For My Dog, Rocco

First, gather kisses and cuddles
Stir in a box of tasty treats
Season with games of fetch in the garden
Add a pinch of kindness
Pour in a pint of dreaded car rides
And whisk in some endless sleeping
Blend in playfulness and silliness
Then warm gently by shouting, "Let's go for a walk!"

Fraser Mennie
Westhill Academy, Westhill

A Recipe For My Cat, Willow

First, gather sleepiness and calmness
Stir in a gallon of adventures to show craziness
Season with a sprinkle of catnip
Add a pinch of confidence
Pour in a bucket's worth of food
And a whole lot of lying around
Blend in some purring
Then warm gently, by finding the flies that she has chewed up.

Iona Ruby Noble
Westhill Academy, Westhill

This Is Me!

First, gather kindness and happiness
Stir in a bucket of activities
Season with the love of excellent parents
Add a pinch of siblings and running
Pour in a mountain's worth of football
And generosity in sports as well
Blend family and friends, walks and talks
Making funny faces to all.

Demi Omitogun (12)
Westhill Academy, Westhill

This Is Me

First, gather intelligence and loyalty
Stir in a pile of Yu-Gi-Oh! cards
Season with ground-up traffic cones
Add a pinch of resilience
Pour in liquid code
Add some imagination in
Blend helpfulness, martial arts, and the name Bob
Warm using a blazing flame and hope it
doesn't explode.

Dylan Boardman (12)
Westhill Academy, Westhill

A Recipe For My Twin Sister, Daisy

First, gather love and generosity
Stir in a pot of fun and creativity
Season with thoughtfulness and beauty
Add a pinch of kindness
Pour in a tub of music
And a river of Taylor Swift songs
Blend in a mix of football, drawing, holiday and eating
Finally, warm gently with family and friends.

Jemima Mitchell
Westhill Academy, Westhill

A Recipe For Thyself

First, gather cheekiness and sportiness
Stir in boredom and adventure
Season with a game of table tennis
Add a pinch of unfriendliness
Pour in a river's worth of smartness
And a desire to play on my phone
Blend playing, running, jumping and breathing
Then warm gently, by hiding in my room.

Aaron Zhaodi Li McKay (12)
Westhill Academy, Westhill

This Is Me

First, gather friends, fun and silliness
Stir in a tub of energy and intelligence
Season with sleeping and keeping secrets
Add a pinch of joy
Pour in an ocean's worth of helpfulness
and kindness
And the love for football
Blend in sportiness and trust
Then warm gently with excitement.

Scott Donaldson (12)
Westhill Academy, Westhill

A Recipe For Our Chicken, Maggie

First, gather calmness and pecking
Stir in a bit of chasing other chickens
Season with adventures
Add a pinch of knowing to bring food
Pour in an ocean's worth of being pampered
And a reason to respect
Blend fearless, shaking and screaming
Then warm gently with jumping on a log.

James Grant (12)
Westhill Academy, Westhill

My Rabbits, Smudge And Fudge

First, gather cuddles and kisses
Stir in their favourite chewing toys
Season with lots of digging holes and chewing toys
Add a pinch of cuteness and love
Pour in pellets, grass, vegetables and sleep time
Blend in tummy tickles and happiness
Then warm gently with love and attention.

Aaron Kidd (12)
Westhill Academy, Westhill

This Is Me

First, gather kindness and fun
Stir in Mum, Dad, and brother
Season with my amazing friends
Add a pinch of helpfulness
Pour in an ocean's worth of noisiness
And a sprinkle of happiness
Blend in tennis, games, parties, and sports
Then warm gently by adding lots of love.

Filip Micak (12)
Westhill Academy, Westhill

A Recipe For Me

First, gather sportiness and football
Stir in PE and football boots
With a tablespoon of football kits
Add a pinch of consideration
Pour in kindness
And tackling viciously and running fast
Blend in Greggs sausage roll, chips and a Sunday roast
Then bake until done.

Harley Masson (12)
Westhill Academy, Westhill

This Is Me

First, gather laziness and craziness
Stir in a lot of laughter
Season with tons of dancing
Add a pinch of grumpiness
Pour in a bit of eating and sleeping
And a smile for days on end
Blend in hanging out with friends every day
And there you have it, the best recipe ever!

Mylah Forrest (12)
Westhill Academy, Westhill

A Recipe For My Cat, Tom

First, gather playfulness and curiosity
Stir in some tuna and pets
Season with playing with string
And a pinch of being active
Pour in love for my older brother
And lots of chin scratches
Blend hunting, gentleness and being nervous
Then warm gently by having a good nap.

Sam Lamont (12)
Westhill Academy, Westhill

A Recipe For My Mum

First, gather generosity and kindness
Stir in a bunch of baking
Season with a bundle of cuddles
Add a pinch of dreams
Pour in a bubble of laughter
And a gallon of family love
Blend tickles, fun and a helping hand
Then warm gently with her loving
home-cooked meals.

Joe Pirie (11)
Westhill Academy, Westhill

A Recipe For My Bunnies, Mina And Harley

First, gather cuddliness and sleeping
Stir in big mountains of fluff
Season with hopping around
Sprinkle a pinch of toys and lots of cuddles
And whip up a bunch of attention
Blend big snuggles and lots of snuggles
Then warm gently, with tons of kisses.

Emily Gomez (12)
Westhill Academy, Westhill

This Is Me

First, gather kind and uplifting
Stir in a load of movies
Season with watching me play fitba
Add a pinch of generous
Pour in a truckload of trust
And lovely drives together
Blend in some running with a group
Then warm gently by chatting at night.

Brodie Lawson
Westhill Academy, Westhill

A Recipe For Dylan

First, gather football and my phone
Stir in video games
Season with chilling with my family
Add a pinch of time out with my friends
Pour in a sea of fun
And a bit of kindness
Blend with hard work
Then warm gently by watching the football.

Dylan Smith (12)
Westhill Academy, Westhill

A Recipe For My Great-Grandad Harry

First, gather mindfulness and happiness
Stir with his favourite stuff
Season with love
Add a pinch of songs
Pour in lightness
And more love
Blend in with everything he loves
Then warm gently by making him happy.

Zara Hogg
Westhill Academy, Westhill

A Recipe For Inga

First, gather cuteness and mischief
Stir in sausages, playing and toys
Season with energy
Add a pinch of walks and scratches
Pour in a load of digging and laziness
Blend sleep, barking and being annoying
Then warm gently by tininess.

Niall Munro
Westhill Academy, Westhill

A Recipe For My Dog, Izzy

Drizzle chaos and whisk in cuddles
Measure a tablespoon of kisses and paws
Blend in soft and fluffy fur
A pinch of affection to balance it out
Pour in unpredictability and clinginess
And to stabilise, grate in walks and hyperactivity.

Grace Proud
Westhill Academy, Westhill

A Recipe For Me

First, gather football and agility
Stir in a lot of good looks
Season with some humour
Add a pinch of table tennis
Pour in some family and friends
Measure some kindness
Blend with so much energy
Serve with family Christmas.

Noah Strand (12)
Westhill Academy, Westhill

This Is Me

First, gather dreams and joy
Stir in a good book and great outdoors
Season with ginger and pumpkin
Add a pinch of music
Pour in an ocean of energy
And lots of gold
Blend in creativity, freedom
And happiness and colour.

Eliana Svensen (13)
Westhill Academy, Westhill

A Recipe For My Dog, Benji

First, gather goofy and bubbles
Stir in long walks in the wilderness
Season with silly spinning
Add a pinch of meeting new dogs
Pour in tons and tons of toys
Add loads of cuddles with grandparents.

Ewan Anderson (12)
Westhill Academy, Westhill

This Is Me

This is me, I love to ski
I'm as happy as can be
As crazy as a bee
Lazy like a sleepy sloth
As loud as a lion
Hungry like a hippo
This is me and you can't change me.

Caleb Humphrey (12)
Westhill Academy, Westhill

What A Mirror Sees

What a mirror sees isn't the real me
It doesn't show what's inside
And that's what makes me shine!
It doesn't show my love for music
It doesn't show my dance
It doesn't show my love for art
It doesn't show my prance!

It doesn't show my kindness
It doesn't show my love
It doesn't show my friendship
It doesn't show enough!

Poppy Grocott (8)
Whitchurch Primary School, Whitchurch-On-Thames

When I Grow Up...

When I grow up
I don't want to be an astronaut
Flying high in space
Looking down on Earth
To see my favourite place

When I grow up
I don't want to be a doctor
Giving love and care
To my many patients
So they avoid despair

When I grow up
I don't want to be an artist
Drawing my own land
Painting, mixing, doodling
Creating with my hand

When I grow up
I don't want to be a detective
And uphold the law

Solving crimes, helping people
Searching and so much more

When I grow up
I don't want to be a footballer
Booting the ball to the sky
Playing for my country
Lifting trophies up high

When I grow up
I don't know what I want to be
But I do know
I just want to be me.

Constance Berrington (11)
Whitchurch Primary School, Whitchurch-On-Thames

Changemaker

I am a drop in the ocean
A star in the galaxy
A fledgling, ready to fly
One dot in a beautiful picture
I am a tiny part of the universe
And I'm ready to burst

So many words to say
And songs to sing
Things coming my way
So many thoughts to think
And dreams to hatch

But I'm a wave that's about to break
A bird ready to soar
A star that's shining brighter

One drop in a wave can rock the ocean
One bird in flight can shake the sky
One person can spark a revolution
One idea can change the world

That's me
A wave about to break
A bird about to soar

I'm a changemaker.

Pippa Stringer-Smith (10)
Whitchurch Primary School, Whitchurch-On-Thames

This Is Me...

This is me
I like food
I have a brother and sister
My brother is really rude!

This is me
I like chess
My mum's a bit round
But she still fits in a dress

This is me
I like tea
My dad's really funny
And he's got ADHD

This is me
I like trees
I'm going to stop pollution
I'm going to save the bees

This is me
I am nine

Life can be hard
But I'll be fine.

Reuben Lay-Sans (9)
Whitchurch Primary School, Whitchurch-On-Thames

I Can Do Anything

I can do anything
I could be a pirate
I could be a farmer
I can do anything
Even be an astronaut!

Though more than anything
I'd like to be the president
And to all girls, I would say
"Stand out, be proud
But most importantly, be yourself
You can do anything too."

Ella Skelhorn (7)
Whitchurch Primary School, Whitchurch-On-Thames

All Of The Dogs

Cute dogs, fluffy dogs
Bulldogs, tall dogs
Small dogs, puffy dogs
And all dogs

Some dogs like food
Some dogs like cuddles
That dog's just pooed!
He must be muddled

Some dogs guide
Some dogs herd sheep
Other dogs just hide
And all dogs love sleep.

Jay Jennings (8)
Whitchurch Primary School, Whitchurch-On-Thames

I Am Hugo!

I am Hugo
And I am fun
I come up with
Lots of puns

I am Hugo
And I am cool
I like seeing
My friends at school

I am Hugo
And I am smart
I like maths
PE and art

I am Hugo
That's for sure
I can't think
Of anymore.

Hugo Lay-Sans (7)
Whitchurch Primary School, Whitchurch-On-Thames

My Teddies

My teddy is called Ted
And she likes to sleep in bed
Polly is my poodle
She loves chicken noodles
My penguin is called Clover
She likes a sleepover
Sammy is my rainbow bear
She has lovely fluffy hair
My favourite dog is called Spots
It looks like she has chickenpox.

Margaret Campbell (7)
Whitchurch Primary School, Whitchurch-On-Thames

This Is Me

I see a light
Shining bright
At the end of time
I walk across the corridor
I reach out, trying to grab it
But then it disappears
And the world
Goes blank
And in the distance
You can see me
Shining bright
Like a star
In the sky.

Micaela Osan (10)
Whitchurch Primary School, Whitchurch-On-Thames

This Is Me!

My name is Arthur
I like to ride my bike
I would rather ride my bike than hike
I am seven years old
I like to play with Lego
Less than riding my bike
Never put a spike in my bike!

Arthur Gammin (7)
Whitchurch Primary School, Whitchurch-On-Thames

This Is Me

This is me.
Sometimes I can be happy
Creative and a little crazy.
I like to be right and to fight
But I hate it when other people are right.
I'm good at a gymnasium
And at being a lazyium
But that doesn't stop me from being amazingium!
Sometimes I cry
But that doesn't stop me from being alive.
I love to eat ice cream
Whilst at the beach
And to swim with fish
And to eat chips!
I'm a gymnastics champ
I love springboards and handsprings.
Sometimes it's hard
Sometimes it's impossible.
On the beam I try my hardest
On the bar, I fly through the air.

Sometimes things are hard
But that doesn't stop me from being me!

Eva Shepherd (11)
York Steiner School, Danesmead

I Have An Egg

I have an egg
I stole it from Greg
Greg was going to eat it
I'm going to keep it
Later that night
Egg was in a fright
I smelt steam
I heard a scream
I walked down the stairs
To Greg's evil lair
Greg was standing there
With his evil glare
Yolk in his hair
Eggshell on the floor
He poached my egg
I'll poach his soul.

Gwen Lavan (11)
York Steiner School, Danesmead

This Is Me

This is me
I am brave
Adventurous
And hyper
When I am with the right people
I can laugh and fight
But that doesn't stop me in life
My future waits
While I get through school
I also like footie and pool
I am a basketball champ
I love hearing the net swoosh
The shoes squeaking
And I just remember
This is just me.

Honey Stewart (12)
York Steiner School, Danesmead

A Minecraft Poem

The clash of swords on shields
Fire and arrows flying overhead
People falling dead on the ground
Boom! goes the red box
Everything goes black...
"Wake up, we won!" says a voice
I'm in a red bed
I'm on half-health
I don't know where I am
My friend's base, I think
My armour on a stand
And my sword in a frame
Wait, did we... We won!

George Aston (12)
York Steiner School, Danesmead

Furious Is Me

Furious is me
Yet I can't help it
Not that it was wrong that I met a...
No, not yet, it was a bit of a

Chestnut going
Up and down, but
Those who think me crazy can go
Hi, I made a mistake. Don't go, I was going to
Embark on a journey. But I
Lit upon it, yet it
Lit me up inside and then I said goodbye.

Fynn Cuthell (11)
York Steiner School, Danesmead

Roblox

I am a maker
I am an undertaker
Fiddling with my stuff
Fixing all my luck
Making all my games mods
MacBook goes *boop boop*

Walking down my city
Making it look pretty
Spending all my lofty
On my famous Gucci
Halloween upgrades
Always kind of spooky
Playing Adopt Me
With my friend Archie.

Diego Del Castillo (11)
York Steiner School, Danesmead

The Flying Gooseman

The first time I saw the Class 20
I thought, *best locomotive in the world!*
The cab's curve
And its small window
To the side, not the front
The chop of the engine
Three rounds for a heavy load
Slowly, slowly
Two rounds, nice and steady
One, let's go
Fast!
This is me!

Aleksander O'Brien
York Steiner School, Danesmead

This Is Me

I will jump
I will run
I will glide
Through all the fun
I will make and create
All the stuff I love to do
If I was an eagle
I will fly higher than
The earthly sky
I will sing to all the birds
I rule within
This is me.

Sebastian Tuck-Parzanese (12)
York Steiner School, Danesmead

In A World Of Fantasy

I am a fighter, a Samurai, a swordsman
The gleam of my blade shines through the night
One side sharp, one side soft
The weapon I use is special, but not?
I am different, more cultured, less flashy
I am me and no one else.

Arthur Greenbrown (11)
York Steiner School, Danesmead

Books

A pile of books
A ticket around the world
A diary full of memories
Last summer retold
And in that pile of books
My future is seen
For one of those books
Is written by me.

Lara Joyce-Rodriguez (11)
York Steiner School, Danesmead

I Am Gluten Free!

I am chocolate
I am a cake
I am a brownie
I am gluten-free
Who knows how I feel today?
Who knows how I feel tomorrow?
But after all
This is me!

Eryka Lawson-McMullan
York Steiner School, Danesmead

Who Is She?

Short spiky white hair
Big silver rings
Shiny silver jewellery
And piles of books
She is the person I admire
Who is she?

Matilda McGorty
York Steiner School, Danesmead

Who Am I?

I don't like maths
Yuck!
I love food no matter what
Yum, yum, yum!
I clean the dirty dishes
Scrub, scrub, scrub
Watching The Simpsons I always like
As much as riding my bike!

I play football and Roblox games
I'm a busy bee
My best friend is James
I love kittens
But I can be angry
Like a bear with a sore head
I love being adventurous
And sporty!

Cute, small puppies and big, fast horses for me!
One day, a policeman I will be!

Cian Parry (10)
Ysgol Gynradd Tanygrisiau, Tanygrisiau

Saturday Morning

When I play football in the rain
It's such a pain
The wind is cold on my body
I am colder than everybody
My orange hair waving in the air
Whoosh!
Shots coming in from everywhere
But I did not care
I saved them all
The crowd cheers
Goal!
Goal!
Goal!
The rain kept pouring
And it was quite boring
The ball flew to the top right
I dived with all my might
And saved the shot
I was as muddy as a pig
Rolling in the mud all day

After the game we all celebrate
And rush to go into the car and wait.

Sion Thomas-Humphreys (10)
Ysgol Gynradd Tanygrisiau, Tanygrisiau

Me And My Friends

My name is Nora
I am seven years old
I love kittens and puppies
I hate getting shouted at
I like going to my nan's house

My friends are Willow and Emma Layla
I miss my old school
I miss my friends
I miss my teachers
I miss Maenofferen School

My friends are Nancy, Kiera, Aleia, Catrin and Tomos
I love the outside but I don't like the inside
I like spaghetti bolognese
I made new friends
I don't like things that change
I like animals.

Nora Pitt (7)
Ysgol Gynradd Tanygrisiau, Tanygrisiau

All About Me!

I am as fast as a train
Toot, toot!
I am happy
I am grateful for my teddy bears

I like playing games and watching TV
I really like being with my family

Sometimes I am mad
Or really, really sad
Or even cry like a raincloud
But sometimes I am really, really happy
Like when I see cute puppies
Woof, woof!
I feel over the moon when I smell spaghetti
Bolognese
Yum!
But the best thing of all is the hugs from
My mum and dad.

Jim Bentley (9)
Ysgol Gynradd Tanygrisiau, Tanygrisiau

Happy

Happy Hayleigh
I am happiest having hobbies
Hurtling across the football field with my ball
Playing outside on my bike
Zooming past
Having fun on my phone until...
I am as tired as a dog that's just been for
a long walk
I love the Liverpool football team
And munching on pizza...
I could eat it all day, every day

But... I hate spooky, black spiders
Scary, slithery snakes
Salad and vegetables.

Hayleigh Wilson-Jones (10)
Ysgol Gynradd Tanygrisiau, Tanygrisiau

My Feelings

I feel happy when my mum comes home from work
I feel sick when I go out for a long time with
my friends
I feel mad when I can't get food on my fork
I feel adventurous when I'm making dens

I feel tired after school, like a dog after a long
walk in the park
I feel cautious when I climb very high places
I feel as excited as people in a show when get
home to my dog

I feel a lot of things in my headspace.

Aron Jones (11)
Ysgol Gynradd Tanygrisiau, Tanygrisiau

Gymnastics

G ymnastics is my favourite thing to do
Y es, I love gymnastics day and night
M akes me happy and carried away
N ice round cartwheels round and round
A mazing round-offs flying in the air
S tars are in the Olympics now, will I ever go? I don't know
T urning out I am great
I love gymnastics
C an't
S top!

Emmalayla Bentley (7)
Ysgol Gynradd Tanygrisiau, Tanygrisiau

My Bike

Help! My bike has been stolen
My puppy was running in the garden and playing
"Help! My bike has been stolen!"
"Put the pot over there!" shouted Mum
"Yes, of course"
I went over to put the pot over there in the shed
Where is my bike?
Help! My bike has been stolen
Scared
Angry
Panic

Help! My bike has been stolen!

Owen Jones (10)
Ysgol Gynradd Tanygrisiau, Tanygrisiau

Fears

The wind is howling in the night
I'm sat down full of fright
I start running down the street
I have met my defeat
Enormous spiders are catching up with me
Everything is covered in fallen debris
Will I live to see another day?
I ran into a wet dark alleyway
Wet, green algae racing down the walls
It's like I'm in-between a million wars.

Agathe Griffiths-Bell (10)
Ysgol Gynradd Tanygrisiau, Tanygrisiau

What's Important

I am happy
I am adventurous
My hair is as brown as dirt
I slurp my drink every time I go to a restaurant
My favourite colour is green like mint
I am as messy as a pig
I am tall like a giraffe
I love nature like my cat and dog love me
I care about my friends
I go out to play almost every day
Whatever the weather
I am me!

Esi Tomos (9)
Ysgol Gynradd Tanygrisiau, Tanygrisiau

Likes And Dislikes

I like snakes
I like cats
I like teddies
I like the sun
I like Ferraris
I like my family
I like games
I like noodles
I like to play with my friends
I like to paint
I like to colour
I don't like spiders
I don't like grapes
I don't like apples
I don't like sharks.

Evie Streeter (8)
Ysgol Gynradd Tanygrisiau, Tanygrisiau

My Likes

I like fun football
Goal! Goal! Goal!
I like big fluffy dogs
Ruff! Ruff! Ruff!
I like games galore
Lego, Lego, Lego!
I like the spotty, yellow cheetahs
Shoo! Shoo! Shoo!
I like dinosaurs
Roar! Roar! Roar!
But most of all
I like my kind mam and brilliant dad!

Layton Butters (7)
Ysgol Gynradd Tanygrisiau, Tanygrisiau

Grateful

I am happy that I have a family
And two dogs that are fluffy and puffy
Three guinea pigs, two bunnies and two fish

McDonald's
Yum, yum, yum!
A cuddly Pikachu
Learning maths in school
Liverpool winning
Going on holiday to hot places.
Playing the guitar
And curly hair.

Cian O'Callaghan (9)
Ysgol Gynradd Tanygrisiau, Tanygrisiau

Best And Favourite

Robots are the best
Omelettes are tastiest
Yum
Blox is my favourite toy
Logos are the best
I stay up till midnight drawing
Busy as a bee
The oval is my favourite shape

Best of all Christmas
It's my favourite time of year
I am happy as a pig in mud.

Catrin Hatton (10)
Ysgol Gynradd Tanygrisiau, Tanygrisiau

My Hamster

He nibbles and nibbles while singing me a song
He is happy all day long
But he loves to sleep and sleep
Sometimes he is just right to be hype
His name is Gizmo
He looks like cookie dough
He is the best pet in the world.

James Wakelin (8)
Ysgol Gynradd Tanygrisiau, Tanygrisiau

Me

I love sports and spinning
My worst fear is snakes
I live in a house of eight
Two of them are my siblings
And they drive me crazy
When it's time to get out of bed
I'm lazy.

Lili Thomas (8)
Ysgol Gynradd Tanygrisiau, Tanygrisiau

I Am Me

I am a happy puppy when I have sugar
I almost burst when I saw a racing car
I am sad when my mum goes to work
I am scaredy-cat when I watch scary movies
I am short
I am funny.

Manawydan Roberts (7)
Ysgol Gynradd Tanygrisiau, Tanygrisiau

My Dog

My dog is crazy like a monkey
When I see her after school
Her tail wags and wags all day long
I love her like a best friend
When I see her
She makes me very happy!

Lucy Wakelin (9)
Ysgol Gynradd Tanygrisiau, Tanygrisiau

YoungWriters Est. 1991

YOUNG WRITERS INFORMATION

We hope you have enjoyed reading this book – and that you will continue to in the coming years.

If you're the parent or family member of an enthusiastic poet or story writer, do visit our website **www.youngwriters.co.uk/subscribe** and sign up to receive news, competitions, writing challenges and tips, activities and much, much more! There's lots to keep budding writers motivated!

If you would like to order further copies of this book, or any of our other titles, then please give us a call or order via your online account.

Young Writers
Remus House
Coltsfoot Drive
Peterborough
PE2 9BF
(01733) 890066
info@youngwriters.co.uk

Join in the conversation!
Tips, news, giveaways and much more!

YoungWritersUK **YoungWritersCW** **youngwriterscw**

Scan me to watch the This Is Me video!